AUE PAVILIONS

AUE PAVILIONS

Paul Robbrecht · Hilde Daem

Temporary Buildings for Documenta IX

Verlag der Buchhandlung Walther König
Köln 1994

THE LANDSCAPE, THE PLACE, THE PARK

It was the need for an endless horizon that finally led to building the Aue Pavilions and to giving them an essential place within Documenta IX. An exhibition that wanted to reject any boundary. The Aue Pavilions refer to that horizon, they want to be a visual cause for the flowing of art to the world. No boundaries, yet no center.

The pavilions were built in the immense eighteenth century park of the Friederichs Aue, a park with a formal perspectivistic scheme stretching out along the Fulda River. In the center of this park is the Orangerie. Three alleys radiate from a three-lobed, clover-leaf shaped square. Alleys and canals lead to a pond with a tea pavilion. The garden as a sanctuary for dream and fantasy.

The park is situated in the valley between the Fulda River and the Kleine Fulda, sixteen meters lower than the Kassel city center. The entire garden configuration moves tangentially along with the eighteenth century urbanization of Kassel. From the Friederichsplatz one overlooks the landscape that is formed by successive stratifications. The Aue is always misty and the different plans of tree groupings and water surfaces become more tenuous in the distance. The garden doesn't mark precise borders, imperceptibly it melds into the vast Hessian landscape. In the distance appear the smooth hills of

Lower Saxony and Thuringia: new lands. In respect to the city, the garden stretches out with an inevitable presence, as nature not to be forgotten, unlimited and totally without meaning. Nature that, even if it has been mainly formed by agriculture, still looks like peaceful nature, totally innocent and inhuman. Yet in this quality the landscape is much more authentic than the actual city of Kassel, which doesn't know what to do with itself, with its identity, with history and neither with modern life. A city that is now situated in the geographical center of the reunited Germany. This coincidence of vacuums, the city and the romantic landscape with its constructed naturalness, is the field in which the Documenta had to be played.

Time and again the Friederich's Aue had an important function in the successive editions of Documenta as artists placed works there, most often sculptures. During conversations with the Documenta director Jan Hoet the idea surfaced that this time painting should be shown in the Aue, a direct confrontation between painting and its origin, the landscape. Painting or retinal art: that form of expression that wants to reach the eye first. An art that seduces with its colors and its shameless illusive pursuit, and that ultimately captivates. The idea to hold up paintings as signs to the landscape of the world would be decisive for the further development of ideas around the Aue Pavilions.

Goethes gardenhouse

For the sake of convenience the word 'painting' is here being used for all the art that takes place more or less on a plane and that is hung on the wall. Carelessly, the word embraces paint as well as canvas as well as photograph, drawing, etc. Also, not only exclusively painting would be shown here, but all the art that has in one way or another to do with light, space and landscape: for instance, sculpture that doesn't only manifest itself as form but equally brings out the light maximally.

Along the Kleine Fulda is a slightly undulating, long and narrow area on which there are a few solitary trees. This strip of land is very visible from the upper edge of the slope between the park and the city. The field is situated along the edge of the park and its borders run parallel to the park structure. It is a place where one arrives and sighs:'here I want to build'. Rarely architects of our generation are able to make their choice in such open grounds. We are the generation that has urban chaos as its normal field of activity. In Kassel, a vast valley was lying in front of us, where we could pick exactly that spot that had everything, both interiorly and exteriorly, to express our purpose. With some deference we thought of the great Greek architects who deliberately placed their temples in the landscape, especially those who built the Bassae in the Peloponesos and the temple in Segeste, on Sicily. Those are buildings that exist in nature with an almost evident harmony, yet at the same time provoke a large surprising effect on the viewer. An unexpected sudden appearance.

Maybe we will never again experience the intensity that we experienced while building the Aue Pavilions: the first architectonic act is the choice of the building site. A choice that has been determined by the elements, the natural slope of the grounds, the groups of trees, the water, the horizon with the rising and setting sun. The effect the building would have on the visitor seeing it for the first time. Making architectures is not an innocent spontaneous occupation, on the contrary, it is an activity that is based on evaluation and reflection. Architecture originates for the better part from experience and calculation, and even more from imitation. Yet there is the necessity that the makers of architecture invest their own intimate experiences in the architectonic project, so that the building will have intensity. Contrary to the making of art which makes explicit the artist's interiority in the work of art, in architecture particular energy is dedicated to the hiding of this individuality to bring the architectonic project to the level of recognition. The architect is the restorer of the known.

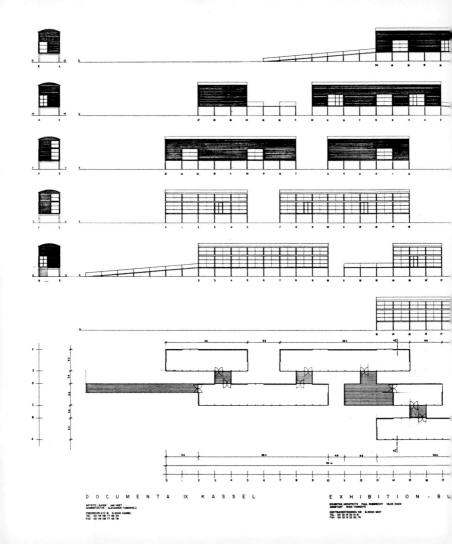

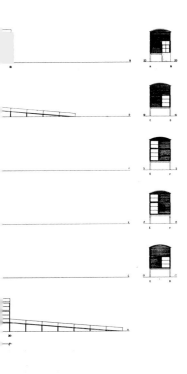

PLAN 1/200

ING KARLSAUE

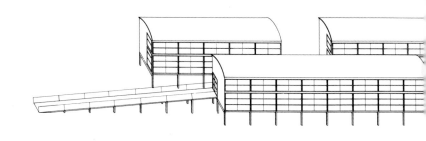

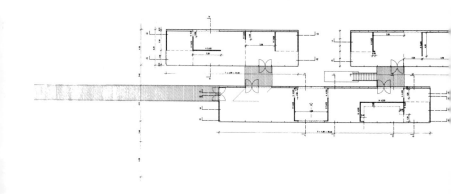

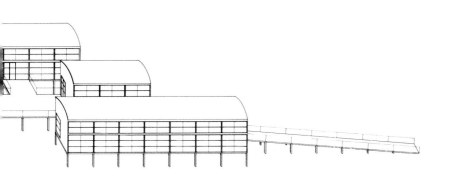

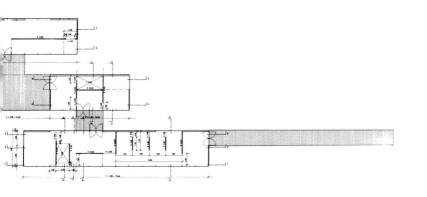

TECHNIQUE

The Aue Pavilions are five different volumes that are supported above the ground by colonnades of steel posts. The pavilions can be reached by sloping planes and they are connected by pontoons.

The pavilions were entirely constructed in a workshop and assembled on the spot. The construction is such that the buildings can be removed and reassembled in another location. An absolute requirement was that there would be as few changes as possible to the existing landscape and the ground profile. Afterwards, everything had to be brought back to its original state.

Each pavilion has a width of 6,30 m and a height of 5,60 m. The floor level is about 2,20 m above the ground. Each space has a fixed modulation with bays of 4,80 m. The five pavilions have different lengths: 33,6 m; 9,6 m; 38,4 m; 38,4 m; 24 m.

The covered surface is 907,2 m2. The total walking circuit is 240 m.

The foundations are prefabricated pads of reinforced concrete with an average dimension of 1,5 m x 1,5 m x 0,4 m. The structure is made from steel I-beams: IPE 330 for the support structure and IPE 240 for the repeated portico elements in the superstructure.

The floors consist of wooden grids covered by wooden boards. The exterior walls are covered by corrugated galvanized steel plates. The plates are attached with self-tapping screws to the steel structure and the steel partitions.

The windows are aluminum frames with single panes of glass.

The space divisions are made of a light lattice covered by plasterboard. There is neither heating nor sanitary installation, there is only natural ventilation through ventilating ducts under the roof.

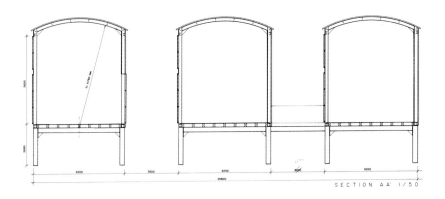

SECTION AA' 1/50

The building is lighted by fluorescent lights. A door knob was designed specially for the Aue Pavilions. It was made of circular iron with a 30 cm diameter and a corner iron 60 cm x 60 cm x 6 cm.
The construction of the Aue Pavilions started in November 1991 with the installation of the prefabricated foundations. The metal skeleton was erected before the winter '91-'92. The pavilions were completed in the spring of 1992. They functioned one hundred days from the 13th of June to the 20th of September. In the fall of 1992 the pavilions were taken down and stored. They will be reassembled in the spring of 1994 in Almere, Flevoland, in the Netherlands, where they will be used as Art Pavilions.

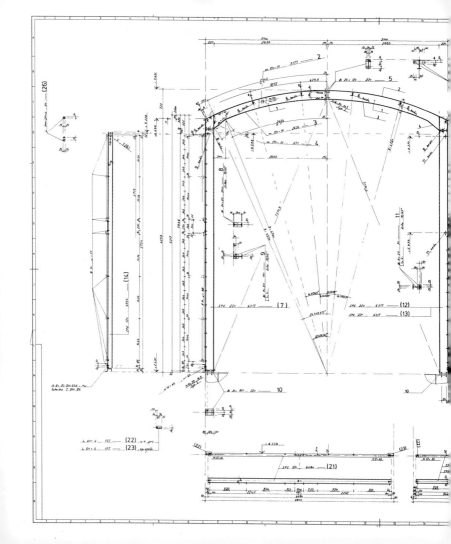

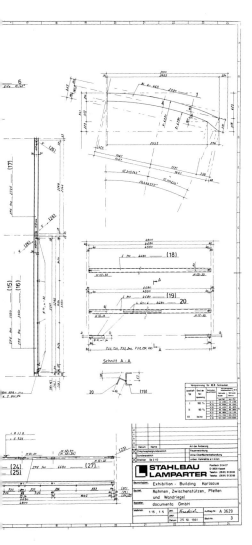

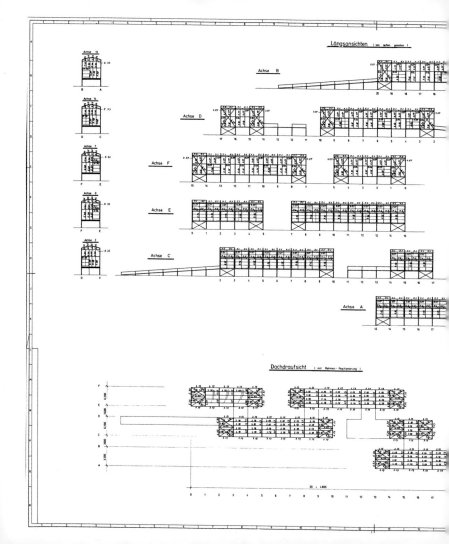

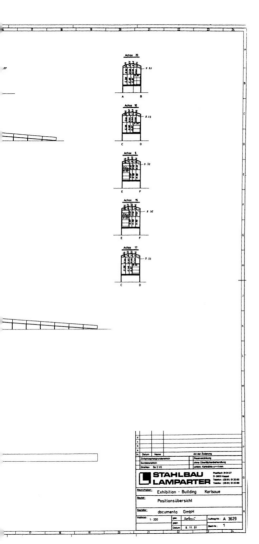

THE CONSTRUCTION

Here, another building comes to mind. Since we saw it for the first time, we haven't succeeded in putting it out of our minds. Goethe's Garden House near the river Ilm in Weimar. We were in Weimar on the occasion of the marathon talks preceding Documenta. In between the sessions we visited the places that reminded of Goethe. In the same period we were reading Johann Peter Eckermann's 'Gespräche mit Goethe' and we also had with us an anthology of his poems. Goethe's Garden House had something irresistible: the elementary block with two storeys and roof presenting itself as an appearance between the trees and the bushes. A house that is the figuration of the house in itself. We hoped that the location of the Aue Pavilions would have the same evidence and that the building

itself would incorporate a similar convergence of structure and shell. Architecture as the ultimate expression of evidence. This was the assignment: to introduce a concentration in a broad landscape, a condensing yet with a great expansive force.

A construction that would dissolve in its surroundings.

Two limiting conditions, namely that the buildings had to serve for only one hundred days and that they had to be realized with a low budget, did not only influence the design of the pavilions, but the entire content as well: transience. What mattered during early talks with the Documenta-team, Jan Hoet, Bart De Baere, Pier Luigi Tazzi and Denys Zacharopoulos, was the idea of 'displacement' as an indication of the actual situation of the artist. While having in the back of their heads all the knowledge and achievements of art, artists are now operating from individual positions.

We used the idea of displacement as an architectonic act, detached from the meaning that was given to it by Jan Hoet and his team. Displacement as a metaphor for trains standing in the landscape, a kind of reverse dynamic of progress of an urban means of transport, a stationary subway train in a romantic landscape, with at the horizon the factory chimneys of Seurat's 'Baignade Asnière'. The garden, a place where all fantasies can be acted out, and where feelings and sentiments are evoked through the suggestive layout. The water as a mirror of the sublime and the forest as the frightening labyrinth. Groupings of trees and bushes set up as scenes that at one time put the stroller in a melancholic mood and in another place transmit feelings of peace, loneliness or heroism. A repertory of feelings in which we, living in the late twentieth century, barely recognize ourselves, or that we have forgotten - or at least the territory that is explored by art.

Finally, we were aware that this group of barracks covered with undulated metal sheets evoked both the image of a concentration camp and the transport to it. Not for one moment did this thought occur during the design, but long before the building was completed, this image imposed itself ineradicably.

We didn't know what our train metaphor so loaded with images could instigate in this area. Probably this building would manifest

the impossibility to establish a place for art. Or maybe this never completed aspiration is the only possible way.

We try to make places where art can be present and this is the parameter for all the buildings we make. All buildings expect the image, the work of art, and hiding in the concurrence of place, image and who is present, is *memorability*.

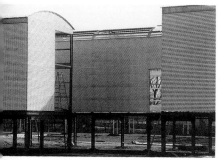

A horse that went to stand, as if by coincidence, in the shade of a tree. The horse has blended with the shadow. Both live together with the tree. (There are few buildings that find their place in such a way.)

Bart De Baere

THE EVENT

And then the first works were hung in the Aue Pavilions.
I remember very clearly they were paintings by Herbert Brandl. And instantaneously we saw that these images were a concentration of color that had to be experienced within the intimacy of Brandl's compartment, yet at the same time they manifested themselves exteriorly, extrovertly. The image against the world, the total landscape. Some artists drilled through the building in order to tie their work of art with the ground (Puryear), in order to establish a relationship between the pavilions themselves (Schaerf) or in order to bring nature in (Merrick).
Raoul De Keyser hung his paintings very low in the empty room. He left little behind, but what was left was tense and brought the viewer to an uncomfortable nervousness. Buphen Kakhar installed himself in his cigarette shop, so that the pavilions were not just a promenade building but a display and a market as well.
With great precision Richter measured his space and the paintings were hung from floor to ceiling. An wood panelled art cabinet in which a series of paintings builds up a complex of interrelations, of which a small floral still life forms the end piece. The viewers directed their looks to the height.

Then, one day in July, the visitors came, they walked through the park and went up the hills, they entered the pavilions. Their walk brought them past the sculptures, the images, the fragmented landscapes. Now and then their looks fell on the trees, on the hill and then again on a painting. A sculpture being reflected in the windows. One was facing the other visitors, in-between the sound of footsteps on the wooden floor. Sometimes face to face, overlapped by the tops of the trees and thousands of leaves. Images covering

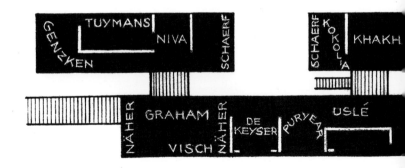

images just as in railroad stations the windows of the departing and the arriving trains. Images projecting themselves on each other. Totally coincidental meetings, totally coincidental connections between the images. Meetings in a subway train but with different light, bedazzlement bathing in light. In the flight the image fastens itself into one's remembrance. I was thinking of Walker Evans' Subway Portraits. Buildings with walls as colorful images, with people walking through, a moment of perfectly transitory unity.

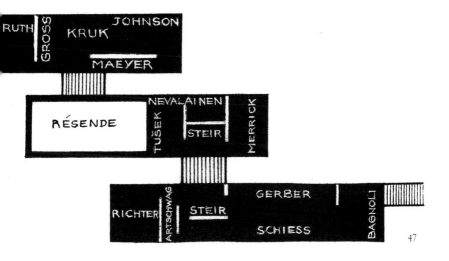

Gaylen Gerber

Adrian Schiess Marco Bagnoli

Pat Steir

Richard Artschwager

Gerhard Richter

GERHARD RICHTER

For Gerhard Richter and with his blessing we constructed a cabinet, the walls of which were covered entirely by American walnut veneer. We made this association after having seen in his studio some of his paintings. Again, Goethe and his mineralogical cabinet came to our minds. The paintings were characterized by the painting of

Blumen, 1992

vertical stripes or a grid structure of horizontally or vertically overlapping color stripes.
Often these abstract paintings had a grated texture.
Sometimes we couldn't rid ourselves of the impression that these abstracts evoked associations of dense vegetations: cattails along the banks of a river. Of the cool lakes of death. Richter organized his paintings in two bands, one on eye level, the other one continuous frieze that was hung high on the wall.
Fourteen abstract paintings, a mirror relief with glass sheets, a small floral still life in the extreme upper corner.

Thom Merrick　　　　　　　　　Pekka Nevalainen

Mitja Tušek

José Resende

Mitja Tušek
Thom Merrick

Marcel Maeyer   Tim Johnson

Bhupen Khakhar

Mariusz Kruk

Michael Gross

Thomas Struth

Vladimir Kokolia

Eran Schaerf

Thomas Struth

Portraits of his friends

Juan Uslé   Herbert Brandl

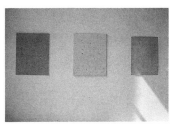

Raoul De Keyser

Martin Puryear   Christa Näher

RAOUL DE KEYSER

Raoul De Keyser's room was in every aspect the opposite of a defined enclosed art cabinet. Glass on two sides, and two entrances. On the two remaining walls, five paintings, three on canvas and two on cardboard, were hung. The paintings had clear ivory backgrounds and were partially smeared with black splotches of paint. Sometimes the surfaces would gleam under the strong incidence of shafts of light. Not for one single moment did this painting attach itself to the place, and on the pictorial field itself the organization of the dark paint splotches was extremely precarious. A wooden bench was giving the viewer some hold and a notion of site. A slatted bench for second class travelers.

DAN GRAHAM

Dan Graham's parallelogram shaped pavilion invested a diagonal relation in the linearly complex of the Aue Pavilions. The work in-between passage, bridge, window, wall, room, mirror and tool.

Henk Visch   Isa Genzken

Isa Genzken

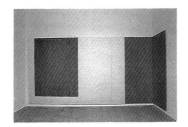
Jussi Niva

Luc Tuymans

ISA GENZKEN

Through the windows one saw barely a thing, or at least nothing special, the ceiling, sky, trees ... fragments of the outer wall, they didn't describe something that demanded attention or that quieted down into a framed image. The sculptures bind their surroundings, as a temporary condensing.
This is however not an intangible connection, an establishment, since when one looks at them thoughts flee to other places, to all remaining imaginable places.
The resin windows are luminescent, a radiation one also experiences in the city at dusk. The glow of curtain walls through which one perceives the interiors, or sometimes completely looks through to the other side.
One looks at these sculptures and thinks one can see the whole world, life, and as usual the light one approaches is elusive.

THIERRY DE CORDIER

De Cordier's scriptorium was hidden in the tops of the surrounding bushes and overlooked the site of the Aue Pavilions with the busy crowds of people.
This place withdrew and raised itself. The shelter and the observation post of the individual. The position of a completely solitary artistic calling, with an inaudible message.

PLACE OF DESTINATION

The Dutch town of Almere in Flevoland is giving a place and a destination to the Aue Pavilions, which in the meantime have been taken down and stored. There as well, they would serve as art

pavilions in a landscape that is in the process of being made. Almere is a town that was founded as a growing pole in the new polders, on land that has been won from the sea.

Yet, there as well, the building will retain its temporary character, even maybe waste away into a rusted steel construction. And there, at times, it will be absorbed by mist and thinness.

BIBLIOGRAPHY

1992	R.& m' Balau *Documenta 9: Architectuur op haar plaats. Displacement, interview met Paul Robbrecht*. A + Architektur, 119, 6/92 R.& m' Balau *Documenta 9: l'architecture A sa place. Displacement. Interview de Paul Robbrecht*. A + Architekture, 119, 6/92
1992	Ludo Beckers *Een andere Visie op de Documenta*. Kunstbeeld, May 1992
1992	Jan Braet *Rondom rend de toren*. Knack, May 6-12, 1992
1992	Jan Braet *Op het randje*. Knack. June 24-30, 1992
1993	Jan Braet *Zacht bekleed met licht, gesprek met Paul Robbrecht en Hilde Daem*. Knack, August 18-24, 1993
1992	Benjamin H.D. Buchloh *Gerhard Richter und die Allegorie des Abstrakten Kabinetts*. Texte zur Kunst, December 1992
1992	Laurens De Keyzer *In de rijkdom van de armoede*. De Gentenaar, June 9, 1992
1992	Laurens De Keyzer *Kassel, de kijker maakt de Kunst*. De Gentenaar, June 19, 1992
1992	Sylvain De Bleeckere *Documenta IX: een gedachten-gang*. Streven, September 1992
1994	Emmanuel Doutrieux *en flandre*. L'architecture d'aujourdhui april '94, n° 292
1986	Marc Dubois *De drang om met architectuur bezig te zijn. Jonge architecten in Belgie*. Stichtings Architectuurmuseum 1986
1992	Marc Dubois *Documenta IX Kassel Aue Paviljoenen van de Architecten Paul Robbrecht en Hilde Daem*. Stichting Architectuurmuseum, July-August-September-October-November, 1992, 92/03-04
1992	Marc Dubois *Tijdelijk Tentoonstellingspaviljoen voor Documenta IX*. Archis, August, 1992
1993	Marc Dubois *Tijdelijk Tentoonstellingspaviljoen voor Documenta IX*. Vlaanderen, March-April, 1993
1993	Marc Dubois *Belgio Architettura, gli ultimi vent'anni*. Electa, 1993

1994	Frederick Hossey *Maison-Galerie Du Grand Art*. L'événement immobilier 85, février 1994
1993	Steven Jacobs *Onvergetelijke Plaatsen*. De Witte Raaf, May 1993
1992	Rik Nijs *Kassel i padiglioni nell'Aue Park*. Domus 741, September 1992
1992	Christos Papoulias *Documenta IX: Under construction*. Tefchos International Review of Architecture, Art and Design 8/1992
1992	Stéphane Penten *Documenta: la polémique a Kassel*. La Libre Belgique, July 16, 1992
1987	Paul Robbrecht *De plaats van de kunst* Vlees en Beton 8, 1987
1991	Paul Robbrecht *Bilder, vorübergehend an eine Wandt gelehnt*. Exhibition catalogue Raoul De Keyser, Kunsthalle Bern and Portikus, Frankfurt, 1991
1991	Paul Robbrecht *The surfaces of the late Twentieth Century* Architecture Now Arcam Pocket, Amsterdam 1991
1992	Paul Robbrecht and Hilde Daem *A Place of Art: Brief* Introduction to the Exhibition Architecture and the temporary Aue Pavilions. Documenta catalogue Part I, Kassel, 1992
1993	Paul Robbrecht *Nieuwe Beelden. Raamsculpturen van Isa Genzken. New Sculptures. Window Structures by Isa Genzken*. Exhibition catalogue Middelheim Biennale, Antwerpen 1993
1992	Dieuwke Van Ooij *Als je in het kunstwerk zit vergeet je de architectuur*. Trouw, July 9, 1992
1992	Janneke Wesseling *Hoog spel in het Fridericianum*. NRC Handelsblad, June 19, 1992
1992	*Infiltraciones Pabello Temporales para Documenta IX*. Quaderns 195
1993	*Einfaches Bauen Ausstellungspavillons in Kassel*. Detail serie 1993/1
1994	Frederick Hossey *Maison-Galerie Du Grand Art*. L'événement immobilier 85, février 1994
1994	Bart Vervaele *Paul Robbrecht & Hildedaem, Raakvlakken tussen Armitectuur en beeldende Kunsten* Leuven 1993–1994
1992	*Waggons im Park*. Bauwelt 23, June 12, 1992

BIOGRAPHIES

HILDE DAEM
born December 12, 1950
1975: architect's diploma
Apprenticeship with Francis Serck
1983: Studies Graphic design

PAUL ROBBRECHT
born October 28, 1950
1974: architect's diploma
Apprenticeship with Marc Dessauvage and Francis Serck
1979: laureate of the "Grand Prix de Rome" for architecture theoretical design on conceptuality and satisfaction in architecture
1980: laureate of the Godecharle Contest for Architecture Project for the restructuring of the Muide, the port area in Ghent.
Teaching assignments:
architecture criticism at the Koninklijke Academie voor Schone Kunsten, Ghent, since 1978
interior architecture at the Hoger Architectuur Instituut van de Stad Gent architectonic design
architecture at the Hoger Sint Lukas Instituut, Ghent.

Architectural office with Hilde Daem

ARCHITECTURAL COMPETITIONS ROBBRECHT-DAEM

1984
Honorary distinction "Prix Bonduelle"
project for the design of a square for the St. Macharius area in Ghent
1985
Selected for the third Biennial for Architecture in Venice, Italy. project: "La Rocca di Noale"
1988
Selected for "Drie pleinen – Zes ontwerpers" by "Rotterdam '88, de stad als podium", for the Rotterdam Art Foundation
project: "Bospolderplein"
1993
Selected for a project for a social housing project "de Hollain" in Ghent

EXHIBITIONS AND CATALOGUES ROBBRECHT-DAEM

1981
"Des Rhétoriques aux Lumières", Festival de Saintées, France. Exhibition about the transition of Baroque Architecture and Neo-Classical Architecture.
1983
"Klein openluchtmuseum voor architecten". Exhibition and catalogue for the Stichting Architectuurmuseum, St. Pietersabdij, Ghent
1985
"De woning als architectuurtypologie". Exhibition and catalogue for the Stichting Architectuurmuseum, Museum of Decorative Arts, Ghent
Article in "Vlees en Beton", RUG, Ghent

1985
"Architectuur voor een Zee-land", Middelburg, the Netherlands. Invitation by the Cultural Council of Zeeland for the design of a new pier in Vlissingen.
Vlissingen and Museum for Contemporary Art, Ghent
1985
Third Biennial for Architecture, Venice
Exhibition and catalogue
1988
"Drie pleinen – Zes ontwerpers", Rotterdam, The Netherlands.
Exhibition and catalogue
1989
"Cabinet for a Doctor", collaboration with Juan Muñoz, Galleria Marga Paz, Madrid, Spain
1989
"De architectuur en het beeld – Architecture and Image", deSingel, Antwerp
Exhibition and catalogue

GUEST LECTURES - LECTURES - PUBLICATIONS

1983
Guest lecturer at the Academy for Architecture, Amsterdam
1985
Guest lecturer at the Academy for Architecture, Tilburg, The Netherlands

1980
"Andreo Palladio Architetto"
Lecture and publication of the WISH-Bulletin,
Hoger Architectuur Instituut, Ghent

1980
"De gewijzigde betekenis van het Rationalisme in de hedendaagse architectuur"
Lecture and publication, Gewad, Ghent
1983
"Verschijnen en verdwijnen in de Villa in de Veneto"
Lecture at the NHIBS-School for Architecture, Antwerp
1984
"Over het beleid aangaande de Architectuur in Belgie"
Lecture and bulletin, Bruges
1984
"Het binnen van de Palladiaanse Villa, over de positie van de Architectuur ten aanzien van de Kunst"
Lecture WISH – Hoger Architectuur Instituut, Ghent
1986
"Eigen Werken". Lecture at the Catholic University, Leuven
1989
"De architectuur en het beeld"
Catalogue deSingel, Antwerp
1985
"Quand on n'a pas ce qu'on aime, on aime ce qu'on a"
Miel De Kooning – Vlees en Beton 4
1986
"Architectuur voor een Zee-land"
Guy Châtel – Vlees en Beton 5
1987
"De plaats van de Kunst"
Paul Robbrecht – Vlees en Beton 8

EXHIBITION CONCEPTS ROBBRECHT-DAEM

1986
"Initiatief 86"
Selection of Kasper König, commissioned by Kasper König
Exhibition architecture, Sint Pietersabdij, Ghent
1987
Exhibition space for the University Campus " De Overpoort", RUG, Ghent, commissioned by Jan Hoet, director of the Museum for Contemporary Art
1986
"Ontwerp voor een Horta-tentoonstelling in Tokyo 1988", commissioned by Europalia, St. Lucasarchief, Brussel.
1987
"Wall for a Painting — Floor for a Sculpture", in collaboration with Isa Genzken, René Daniëls, Cristina Iglesias, Philippe Van Snick, commissioned by Foundation De Appel, Amsterdam
1989
"De architectuur en het beeld", deSingel, Antwerp
1991-92
Documenta IX — 1992, Kassel, commissioned by Jan Hoet. The Aue Pavilions.
1992
Funicular-house for Juan Muñoz, Barcelona
1994
Museography and exhibition architecture for the museum of central Africa Tervuren, Brussels

ARCHITECTURAL REALIZATIONS AND PROJECTS

1979-1982
De Mol House, Kortrijk
1984-1992
Interventions in Mys House, Oudenaarde
1988
Interventions in De Smet House, Ghent
1988-1989
BAC Bank Agency, Kerksken
1989-1991
Meert-Rihoux Penthouse and Art Gallery, Brussels, with a collaboration by Isa Genzken
1989-1990
Extension De Clercq House, Bruges
1991
Marien-Meert apartment, Knokke
1990-1991
Interventions in Vandenabeele House, Ghent
1990-1992
Lannoo House, Sint-Martens-Latem
1990-
Restructuring Warehouse Katoen Natie, Antwerp, with collaboration by Cristina Iglesias
1990-1993
Hufkens Art Gallery and House, Brussels, in collaboration with José Van Hee
1991-1992
Aue Pavilions for Documenta IX, Kassel
1991-1992
Laboratory for Medical Research Innogenetics, Zwijnaarde, Ghent

1991-
Laboratory and Farmhouse for Plant Genetic System, Asper, Deinze
1991-
Apartment Buildings "De Kadehuizen", Coupure, Ghent
1991-
Interventions Ghekiere House, Ghent
1991-1992
Bonne-Daem House and Doctor's Practice, Brecht
1992-
Daem House, Westouter
1992-
Exhibition Space for Ulrich Rückriem, Ben Ahin
1993-
Muyldermans-De Cuypere House, Grimbergen
1993-
Collaboration with Ulrich Rückriem on redevelopment project for Place Schumann, Brussels
1993-
Interventions in De Causmaecker House and Pharmacy, Lokeren
1993-
Shop premises, Cologne
1993-
Porch, Museum voor Schone Kunsten, Ghent
1994
Pfeiffer-offices, Leipzig
1994
Carpentier-De Sauter House, Tielt
1994
Ghekiere House, Sint-Martens-Latem
1994
Daem House, Lede

PHOTOGRAPH
Kristien Daem p. 36-37-38-40-44-51-56-58-59-62-63-68-69-74
Ronny Heirman p. 80-81
Benjamin Katz inside cover and p. 35
Attilio Maranzano cover and p. 5-44-53-75
Peter Nielsen: p. 84
Dirk Pauwels reproductions on p. 48-49-54-55-57-60-61-66-67-70-71-72-73-79
Johannes Robbrecht p. 28-29-30-31-32-33-34-39-42-43-50-77
Paul Robbrecht p. 83
Thomas Struth p. 64-65
Winfried Waldeyer p. 6-24-25-27

THANKS TO
Frank De Baere, Sofie Delaere, Brigitte D'hoore, Els Claessens, Wim Cuyvers, Marleen Goethals, José Van Hee and Hugo Vanneste

© 1994 Paul Robbrecht and Hilde Daem
Verlag der Buchhandlung Walther König, Köln

Concept: Paul Robbrecht, Hilde Daem
Design and Layout: Sony van Hoecke, Ghent
Translation: Kaatje Cusse, Brussels

All rights reserved

Typeset: Neusatz GmbH, Cologne
Lithography: Miess GmbH, Cologne
Production: Franz Paling, Cologne

ISBN 3-88375-192-8
Printed in Germany

994/69
28,-